BY JIM GIGLIOTTI

★ Houston Texans ★ Indianapolis Colts ★ Jacksonville Jaguars ★ Tennessee Titans ★

Published by The Child's World®
1980 Lookout Drive
Mankato, MN 56003-1705
800-599-READ
www.childsworld.com

The Child's World®: Mary Berendes, Publishing Director
The Design Lab: Kathleen Petelinsek, Design
Editorial Directions, Inc.: Pam Mamsch and E. Russell Primm,
Project Managers

Photographs ©: Robbins Photography

Library of Congress Cataloging-in-Publication Data
Gigliotti, Jim.
  AFC South / by Jim Gigliotti.
    p. cm. Includes bibliographical references and index.
  ISBN 978-1-60973-129-8 (library reinforced : alk. paper)
 1. American Football Conference—Juvenile literature.
2. Football—Southern States—Juvenile literature. I. Title.
  GV950.7.G538 2011
   796.332'640973—dc22   2011007150

Printed in the United States of America
Mankato, MN
April, 2012
PA02132

TABLE OF
CONTENTS

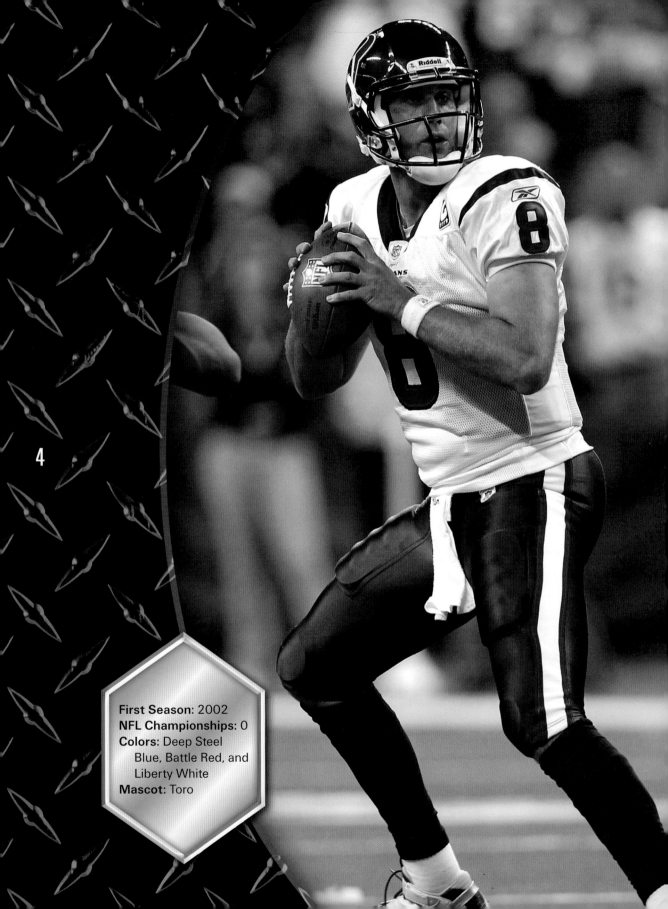

4

First Season: 2002
NFL Championships: 0
Colors: Deep Steel
  Blue, Battle Red, and
  Liberty White
Mascot: Toro

★

HOUSTON
TEXANS

ON THE WAY UP

Most NFL **expansion teams** struggle in their first year. The Houston Texans were no exception. They won only four games in 2002. But the team did have one incredible moment that season—an opening-game victory over the Dallas Cowboys. Houston scored a touchdown a little more than a minute into its very first game and went on to beat its in-state rival 19–10.

In recent seasons, the team has begun to look like a playoff contender. In 2009, the Texans won more games than they lost for the first time in their history and narrowly missed out on the playoffs. The team also boasted one of the NFL's top offenses. If the defense can catch up, watch out!

Quarterback Matt Schaub was the 2010 Pro Bowl MVP.

HOME FIELD

The Texans' Reliant Stadium was the first NFL stadium to feature a **retractable** roof. The roof can be opened or closed on game days, depending on the weather. The team has until 90 minutes before kickoff to decide if they want a roof or not. After that, the team has to stick with its choice no matter what!

BIG DAYS

* After the Houston Oilers moved to Tennessee in 1997, the football-crazed city was without a team until the Texans came along in 2002.
* Houston scored a touchdown after only three plays and a penalty in its first game against Dallas.
* The Texans struggled on offense their first year. Against powerful Pittsburgh, they managed only 47 yards the whole game. The Steelers gained 422 yards. Amazingly, the Texans still won 24–6 by returning two interceptions and a fumble for touchdowns.
* In late 2009, the Texans won three games in a row and had a chance to finish with a winning record for the first time. But the mighty New England Patriots stood in their way. Matt Schaub passed for two touchdowns and Arian Foster ran for two more, as Houston rallied to beat the Patriots 34–27.

Houston's Reliant Stadium can hold up to 71,054 fans.

SUPERSTARS!

★

THEN

Kris Brown, kicker: the leading scorer in team history

David Carr, quarterback: the club's first draft pick, was the starting QB for five years

Domanick Williams, running back: 1,000-yard rusher in both 2003 and 2004

★

NOW

Arian Foster, running back: undrafted player had a surprise breakout season in 2010

Andre Johnson, wide receiver: big and strong, he's twice led the NFL in receiving

Matt Schaub, quarterback: signal caller who engineered the Texans' first winning season

★

STAT LEADERS

(All-time team leaders*)

Passing Yards: Matt Schaub, 14,424

Rushing Yards: Domanick Williams, 3,195

Receiving Yards: Andre Johnson, 9,164

Touchdowns: Andre Johnson, 50

Interceptions: Dunta Robinson, 13

(*Through 2010 season.)

TIMELINE

1999	**2002**	**2003**	**2007**
Houston is awarded an NFL expansion franchise to begin play in 2002.	Texans stun in-state rival Dallas Cowboys to win their first regular-season game.	Domanick Williams becomes the Texans' first 1,000-yard rusher (1,030 yards).	The Texans finish with a .500 record (eight wins and eight losses) for the first time ever.

Running back Arian Foster led the NFL with 1,616 rushing yards in the 2010 season.

2008

Andre Johnson sets a team record by catching 115 passes.

2009

Quarterback Matt Schaub leads the NFL when he passes for 4,770 yards, a club record.

2009

With nine victories in 16 games, the Texans post their first winning season.

10

First Season: 1953
NFL Championships: 4
Colors: Royal Blue and
   White
Mascot: Blue

★

INDIANAPOLIS
COLTS

TALE OF TWO CITIES

The Indianapolis Colts are one of the most **consistent** winning teams in the NFL these days. The club's winning tradition stretches back more than half a century and to a different city. In 1953, the team began as the Baltimore Colts. The Colts featured many great players and won NFL championships in both 1958 and 1959. The 1970 Colts won Super Bowl V.

In 1984, the Colts packed their bags and moved to Indianapolis. Fourteen years later, they chose quarterback Peyton Manning as their number-one draft pick. Since then, they've never looked back. Beginning in 1999, the Colts made the playoffs 11 times in 12 years. They won Super Bowl XLI in the 2006 season!

Receiver Reggie Wayne shares the Colts club record for most receptions in a single game, with 14.

HOME FIELD

In 2008, the Colts moved into Lucas Oil Stadium. Like Reliant Stadium in Houston, it has a roof than can be opened or closed. When the Colts first played with the roof open, it was their first home game in the sunshine in 25 years! They had played under a dome since 1984.

BIG DAYS

★ The 1958 title game between the Colts and the New York Giants was tied 17–17 after four quarters. A lot of people weren't sure what came next. No game had ever gone into overtime before! The Colts won with a touchdown in the extra period.

★ Rookie kicker Jim O'Brien was so nervous in the final seconds of Super Bowl V against the Cowboys that he tried to pick up a blade of grass to **gauge** the wind. But the field was AstroTurf! He made his 32-yard kick anyway, and the Colts won 16–13.

★ The Colts of the early 2000s always seemed to make the playoffs. They just couldn't quite make it to the Super Bowl. But 2006 was their year. Indy edged out the rival Patriots in a **taut** AFC title game, then beat the Chicago Bears 29–17 in the Super Bowl.

The 63,000-seat Lucas Oil Stadium cost about $715 million to build.

SUPERSTARS!

★

THEN

Raymond Berry, **wide receiver**: top pass catcher of his time
Eric Dickerson, **running back**: the most **prolific** NFL rusher of the 1980s
Gino Marchetti, **defensive end**: once voted the top defensive end
of the NFL's first 50 years
John Unitas, **quarterback**: nobody's ever been better at the
two-minute drill

★

NOW

Dwight Freeney, **defensive end**: the Colts' all-time leader in sacks
Peyton Manning, **quarterback**: among the top NFL players
Reggie Wayne, **wide receiver**: topped 1,000 yards for the seventh
year in a row in 2010

★

STAT LEADERS

(All-time team leaders*)
Passing Yards: Peyton Manning, 54,828
Rushing Yards: Edgerrin James, 9,226
Receiving Yards: Marvin Harrison, 14,580
Touchdowns: Marvin Harrison, 128
Interceptions: Bob Boyd, 57

★

(*Through 2010 season.)

TIMELINE

1953
Colts join the NFL and are placed in the Western Conference.

1958
Colts beat the Giants in the NFL's first overtime championship game.

1959
Colts repeat as NFL champs, again defeating the Giants in the title game.

1970
Colts win Super Bowl V over Dallas with a field goal in the final seconds.

Quarterback Peyton Manning has been selected for the Pro Bowl 11 times.

1984	**2002**	**2003**	**2006**
The team moves to Indianapolis.	Colts begin play in the newly formed AFC South Division.	Indianapolis wins the AFC South championship for the first of five years in a row.	Colts defeat the Bears in Super Bowl XLI to win their fourth NFL championship.

First Season: 1995
NFL Championships: 0
Colors: Teal, Black,
and Gold
Mascot: Jaxson
De Ville

★

JACKSONVILLE JAGUARS

INSTANT WINNERS

In 1996, the Jaguars and their fellow expansion team the Carolina Panthers both did something no NFL expansion team before them had ever done. They made the playoffs in only their second season. The Jaguars made it all the way to the AFC Championship Game before suffering a tough loss to the Patriots.

In the years since, the Jaguars have had some really good teams and some not-so-good ones. Mostly, Jacksonville fans remember the great 1999 team. That year, the Jaguars won an NFL-best 14 games during the regular season. But they couldn't get past the division rival Titans. The Titans beat them three times, including once in the playoffs. Jacksonville has returned to the **postseason** twice since then.

Running back Fred Taylor played 11 seasons for the Jaguars before moving to the New England Patriots in 2009.

HOME FIELD

The Jaguars play their home games at EverBank Field. It was built in 1995 on the site of the Gator Bowl, a famous stadium originally built more than 70 years ago. The old stadium wasn't just torn down. Parts of it were included in the new stadium!

BIG DAYS

★ In 1996, their second season, the Jaguars were close to making the playoffs. To advance, they had to beat the Atlanta Falcons in their last regular-season game. When Atlanta's great kicker Morten Andersen missed a short field goal at the end of the game, Jacksonville won 19–17.

★ Running back James Stewart was nicknamed "Little Man," but he played big for the Jaguars in a 1997 game against the Philadelphia Eagles. Stewart scored all five of Jacksonville's touchdowns in a 38–21 victory.

★ The San Francisco 49ers made the playoffs in 1998, but they were no match for the Jaguars in the 1999 season opener. Jacksonville kicked off its 14-win season with a 41–3 victory. It was the most lopsided regular-season win in Jaguars' history.

EverBank field normally holds 67,246 people, but extra seats were added to raise the capacity to more than 82,000 for Super Bowl XXXIX.

SUPERSTARS!

THEN

Tony Boselli, tackle: a Pro Bowl lineman five years in a row
Mark Brunell, quarterback: a good runner and a great passer
Fred Taylor, running back: the team's all-time leader in rushing
yards and TDs

NOW

Maurice Jones-Drew, running back: had a huge season in 2009
when he scored 16 TDs
Rashean Mathis, cornerback: has intercepted more passes than any
other Jaguars player
Josh Scobee, kicker: won a game in 2010 with a 59-yard field
goal as time ran out

STAT LEADERS

(All-time team leaders*)
Passing Yards: Mark Brunell, 25,698
Rushing Yards: Fred Taylor, 11,271
Receiving Yards: Jimmy Smith, 12,287
Touchdowns: Fred Taylor, 70
Interceptions: Rashean Mathis, 29

★

(*Through 2010 season.)

TIMELINE

1995
Jaguars join the NFL as an expansion team.

1996
Jacksonville makes it to the AFC title game in its second season.

1998
Jaguars win their first AFC Central Division championship.

Quarterback Mark Brunell has been playing in the NFL since 1993.

1999

Jaguars win a club record fourteen of 16 regular-season games.

2002

Jacksonville begins play in the newly formed AFC South.

2005

Jaguars win 12 regular-season games to return to the playoffs for the first time in six seasons.

First Season: 1960
AFL/NFL
    Championships: 2
Colors: Navy, Titans
    Blue, Red, and Silver
Mascot: T-Rac

★

TENNESSEE
TITANS

WINNERS BY ANY NAME

The Tennessee Titans' history begins in 1960, with the creation of the American Football League (AFL). One of the league's original teams was the Houston Oilers. The Oilers joined the NFL when the two leagues merged in 1970. In 1997, the Oilers moved to Tennessee. Two years later, the team was renamed the Titans.

No matter their name or location, the team has had success. The Oilers were the AFL champions for the first two years of the league's existence. The team hasn't won a championship since joining the NFL, but they've come close. The Titans made the playoffs six times in a **span** of ten seasons beginning in 1999. That year, the team won the AFC title but lost an exciting Super Bowl game to the St. Louis Rams.

Kicker Rob Bironas had an 84.5 field goal percentage in the first five years of his career.

HOME FIELD

Like the team, the Titans' home field has had a few name changes. When the team first moved into LP Field in 1999, the stadium was called Adelphia Coliseum. Then it became The Coliseum. It became LP Field in 2007 when it was named after a company that makes building products.

BIG DAYS

★ The whole country found out who Earl Campbell was when the Oilers played the Miami Dolphins on a Monday night in 1978. The rookie running back rushed for 199 yards, including a game-clinching 81-yard touchdown in the fourth quarter.

★ Things looked bad when the Titans fell one point behind the Buffalo Bills with just 16 seconds to go in a 1999 playoff game. But after taking a cross-field **lateral** on a kickoff, Kevin Dyson raced 75 yards for the winning touchdown. The play became known as the Music City Miracle.

★ In 2009, Chris Johnson was already having a big year. But it became even bigger in a 17–13 win over San Diego to close the season. Johnson rushed for 134 yards, bringing his season total to 2,006. Only five players before him had ever reached 2,000 yards in a single season.

Up to 69,143 fans can cheer on the Titans at LP Field in Nashville.

SUPERSTARS!

THEN

Earl Campbell, running back: led NFL in rushing three years in a row
Bruce Matthews, offensive line: a fixture on the line, he made
14 Pro Bowls in a row
Warren Moon, quarterback: owns the team game, season, and career
records for passing yards

NOW

Michael Griffin, safety: young **ballhawk** who is emerging as
one of football's top safeties
Rob Bironas, kicker: only NFL player ever to kick eight field goals
in a single game
Chris Johnson, running back: led the NFL with an amazing
2,006-yard rushing season in 2009

STAT LEADERS
(All-time team leaders*)
Passing Yards: Warren Moon, 33,685
Rushing Yards: Eddie George, 10,009
Receiving Yards: Ernest Givins, 7,935
Touchdowns: Eddie George, 74
Interceptions: Jim Norton, 45

(*Through 2010 season.)

TIMELINE

1960
Team begins play as the
Houston Oilers and wins the first
American Football League title.

1961
Oilers win their second AFL
championship in as many
seasons.

1970
Oilers join the NFL and are
placed in the AFC Central
Division.

1997
Houston Oilers move to
Tennessee. Two years later,
they become the Titans.

Running back Chris Johnson is one of just six players in NFL history to gain more than 2,000 rushing yards in a single season.

1999
Titans win the AFC championship for the first time, but lose to the Rams in Super Bowl XXXIV.

2000
Tennessee wins a franchise-record 13 regular-season games for the second year in a row.

2002
Titans win the division title in the first year of the AFC South.

2008
Tennessee wins its first AFC South championship in six years.

STAT
STUFF

★

AFC SOUTH DIVISION STATISTICS*

Team	All-Time Record (W-L-T)	NFL Titles (Most Recent)	Times in NFL Playoffs
Houston Texans	55–89–0	0	0
Indianapolis Colts	470–416–7	4 (2006)	24
Jacksonville Jaguars	138–129–0	0	6
Tennessee Titans	391–408–6	2 (1961)	21

★

AFC SOUTH DIVISION CHAMPIONSHIPS (MOST RECENT)

Houston Texans . . . 0

Indianapolis Colts . . . 7 (2010)

Jacksonville Jaguars . . . 0

Tennessee Titans . . . 2 (2008)

★

(*Through 2010 season; includes AFL statistics.)

AFC SOUTH PRO FOOTBALL
HALL OF FAME MEMBERS

Houston Texans

None

Indianapolis Colts

Raymond Berry, WR
Eric Dickerson, RB
Art Donovan, DT
Weeb Ewbank, Coach
Marshall Faulk, RB
Ted Hendricks, LB
John Mackey, TE
Gino Marchetti, DE
Lenny Moore, WR, RB
Jim Parker, G, T
Don Shula, Coach
John Unitas, QB

Jacksonville Jaguars

None

Tennessee Titans

Elvin Bethea, DE
George Blanda, QB, K
Earl Campbell, RB

Dave Casper, TE
Ken Houston, S
Charlie Joiner, WR
Bruce Matthews, C, T, G
Warren Moon, QB
Mike Munchak, G

NOTE: Includes players with at least three seasons with the team. Players may appear with more than one team.

29

Position Key:
QB: Quarterback
RB: Running back
WR: Wide receiver
C: Center
T: Tackle
G: Guard
K: Kicker
CB: Cornerback
LB: Linebacker
DE: Defensive end
DT: Defensive tackle
TE: Tight end
S: Safety

GLOSSARY

★

ballhawk (BAWL-hawk): a defensive player who often intercepts passes or recovers fumbles

consistent (kuhn-SISS-tuhnt): often performing at the same level

expansion teams (sk-SPAN-shuhn TEEMZ): teams added to an existing league

gauge (GAYJ): to estimate or make a judgment about something

lateral (LAT-ur-uhl): in football, a pass that goes sideways or backward

postseason (POHST SEE-zun): playoffs, including the Super Bowl

prolific (pruh-LIF-ik): very productive

retractable (rih-TRAK-tuh-buhl): capable of being drawn back, as in the roof of a stadium that can slide open

span (SPAN): a length of time

taut (TAWT): tense

FIND OUT MORE

★

BOOKS

Buckley, James Jr. *Scholastic Ultimate Guide to Football*. New York:
Franklin Watts, 2009.

Jacobs, Greg. *The Everything Kids' Football Book*. Avon, MA: Adams
Media, 2010.

MacRae, Sloan. *The Indianapolis Colts*. New York: PowerKids, 2011.

Stewart, Mark. *The Houston Texans*. Chicago:
Norwood House Press, 2009.

Steward, Mark. *The Jacksonville Jaguars*. Chicago:
Norwood House Press, 2009.

Stewart, Mark. *The Tennessee Titans*. Chicago:
Norwood House Press, 2009.

★

WEB SITES

For links to learn more about football visit
www.childsworld.com/links

Note to Parents, Teachers, and Librarians: We routinely verify our Web links to make sure
they are safe and active sites. So encourage your readers to check them out!

INDEX

★

32

ABOUT THE AUTHOR

Jim Gigliotti is a freelance writer based in Southern California. A former editor at the National Football League, he has written more than fifty books on sports for children and adults.